HEROES OF HISTORY

RULERS

Written by **Anita Ganeri**
Illustrated by **Joe Todd Stanton**

PowerKiDS press

Published in 2026 by The Rosen Publishing Group, Inc.
2544 Clinton Street, Buffalo, NY 14224

Copyright © 2015 Weldon Owen.

Created by:
    Author: Anita Ganeri
    Additional text: Nicola Barber
    Illustrator: Joe Todd Stanton
    Additional Illustrations: Katie Abey
    Editorial: Hannah Wilson, Lydia Halliday
    Senior Designer: Krina Patel
    Designer: Natasha Rees
    Index: Vanessa Bird

Cataloging-in-Publication Data

Names: Ganeri, Anita, 1961, author. | Todd-Stanton, Joe, illustrator.

Title: Rulers / by Anita Ganeri, illustrated by Joe Todd-Stanton.

Description: Buffalo, NY : PowerKids Press, 2026. | Series: Heroes of history | Includes glossary and index.

Identifiers: ISBN 9781499454932 (pbk.) | ISBN 9781499454949 (library bound) | ISBN 9781499454956 (ebook)

Subjects: LCSH: Kings and rulers--Biography--Juvenile literature. | Queens--Biography--Juvenile literature. | Heads of state--Biography--Juvenile literature.

Classification: LCC CT104.G364 2026 | DDC 920.02--dc23

All rights reserved.

No part of this book may be reproduced in any form without permission in writing from the publisher, except by a reviewer.

Manufactured in the United States of America

CPSIA Compliance Information: Batch #CSPK26. For further information contact Rosen Publishing at 1-800-237-9932.

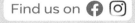

CONTENTS

Introduction	4
Rulers	6
Ramesses II	8
Elizabeth I	14
George Washington	20
Napoleon Bonaparte	26
Glossary	32
For More Information	32
Index	32

INTRODUCTION

History is packed with heroes and heroines who left a lasting legacy behind. Some were larger-than-life characters, born leaders who inspired their followers. Others worked away quietly, shunning the limelight. They earned their fame in different ways – through hard work, determination and, sometimes, sheer luck.

RULERS

History has been shaped by many powerful rulers, leading their country and people in good times and bad. Some were born into power; others grabbed it for themselves. Some have become famous for leading by example, in battle and in peacetime, often at great personal cost. Some have had the gift of being able to inspire their people to great things.

Elizabeth I

Ramesses II

Others have left a long-lasting legacy, in the form of great buildings and monuments, which ensure that their memory never fades.

In this chapter, you can read about a warrior-pharaoh famous for his temples and tombs, a queen who proved to be one of England's toughest rulers, a soldier sworn in as the first president of the United States, and an army officer who created a mighty empire.

George Washington

Napoleon Bonaparte

RAMESSES II
Mighty King

Ramesses II came to the throne of Ancient Egypt at the age of 25, and reigned for an astonishing 67 years. During this time, he fought many battles, founded a new capital city, and built many temples, including the world-famous Abu Simbel.

Ready to rule

Ramesses was born around 1303 BCE. From a young age, he was prepared for his role as king by his father, Seti I. Ramesses accompanied his father when he went on campaigns, and was made a captain in the army when he was only 10 years old. He probably did not lead any troops into battle, but he must have had some serious military training. He certainly went on to become the greatest warrior-pharaoh that Egypt had ever seen.

A long reign

Early on in his reign, Ramesses built a new capital city for himself close to where he was born and raised in the Nile Delta, the area surrounding the mouth of the River Nile. The city, called Pi-Ramesses (House of Ramesses) was famous for its beautiful gardens, orchards, and canals. From here, Ramesses had a handy base for waging war against Egypt's enemies, for leading daring expeditions to win back territories lost by his father, and for securing Egypt's borders.

One of Ramesses' toughest struggles was against the Hittite people, who had built up a great empire in Syria. Ramesses wanted to expand Egypt's borders into Syria, while the Hittites were determined to protect any threat to their trade routes. Things came to a head in 1274 BCE, when Ramesses' mighty army met the forces of the Hittite king, Muwatallis, at the Hittite stronghold of Kadesh.

RAMESSES' EGYPTIAN DIARY

1274 BCE
Kadesh, Syria
We reached Kadesh after a long march and began setting up camp. Two spies told us that the main Hittite army was miles away, so I'd taken only a small guard with me. I should NEVER have listened. In fact, the Hittites were hiding in the city and took us by surprise. We were heavily outnumbered, but, fortunately, reinforcements arrived in the nick of time and saved the day. Sort of. Both sides are claiming to have won, but we're in no state to fight it out again.

About 1259 BCE
Luxor, Egypt
I've finally found time to start work on a grand temple, dedicated to, er, myself (well, there's no point waiting until I'm dead). I'm having the pylons (gateways) and walls decorated with scenes from the Battle of Kadesh, showing us winning a great victory over those pesky Hittites. Hah.

About 1258 BCE
Kadesh (possibly)

I can hardly believe it. After years of fighting, we're finally signing a peace treaty with the Hittites. King Hattusili sent diplomats with the terms inscribed on a silver tablet. I haven't read it all yet, but there are lots of pledges about living in peace and not invading each other's lands. Let's see. For now, I'm having it carved on the walls of my temple at Karnak — at least it shows I'm willing.

1255 BCE
Abu Simbel, Nubia

The queen (Nefertari) and I are here in Nubia for the opening of my new temple at Abu Simbel. It's my biggest and best building project yet. Actually, there are two temples — one for me and one for the queen. Outside my temple, there are four massive statues of me sitting on a throne, carved out of the rock. Pretty awesome, even if I do say so myself.

1250 BCE
Valley of the Queens, Thebes

A very sad day indeed — Nefertari has died. We'd been married for years and I used to call her "the one for whom the sun shines." We've brought her body to the Valley of the Queens, where she'll be buried in the grandest tomb money can buy. I've had the walls painted with scenes from the Book of the Dead — only the best for her.

POWERFUL KINGS

The reign of Ramesses II (1279–1213 BCE) was the second longest in Egyptian history. He was a popular, powerful king. Find out here about other mighty kings who made their mark in history.

Statue of Ramesses II in Luxor, Egypt

Temple builder

Ramesses' reign marked the peak of Egyptian power and prosperity. He spent a huge amount of Egypt's wealth on building projects. He constructed temples, palaces, and monuments across Egypt and Nubia. After his death in 1213 BCE, he was buried in the Valley of the Kings at Luxor.

Louis XIV

Louis XIV succeeded his father at the age of four. His young life was marred by unrest, which left him fearful of rebellion. He set up court at his lavish new palace in Versailles, outside Paris, and ruled with absolute power.

Statue of Louis XIV at Versailles, France

Zulu shield, spear, and club

Shaka Zulu

Shaka, the son of a Zulu chieftain, took power of the Zulu kingdom in South Africa after his father's death in 1816. He armed his warriors with shields and powerful stabbing spears, and began a campaign of terror, overpowering neighboring kingdoms to form a Zulu Empire.

Timeline of royal rulers

1279 BCE
Ramesses II
Egyptian pharaoh begins his 67-year reign of Egypt.

1611
Gustavus Adolphus
Swedish king comes to the throne and begins laying the foundations for the powerful modern state of Sweden.

1643
Louis XIV
Known as the 'Sun King', Louis XIV begins his reign, which, at 72 years and 100 days, is the longest of any monarch in Europe.

1740
Frederick II
Frederick the Great comes to the throne, going on to increase the military power of Prussia and become a noted patron of the arts.

1816
Shaka Zulu
Leader and military innovator takes power. A cruel tyrant, he is murdered by his half-brother in 1828.

ELIZABETH I
Powerful Queen

Late in 1558, on the death of her half sister Mary, Elizabeth I came to the English throne. Shrewd, intelligent, and ruthless, she soon established herself as one of England's greatest rulers, and her 45-year reign is seen as a golden age in English history.

Life and death

Elizabeth was born in Greenwich, London, on September 7, 1533. She was the daughter of the great Tudor king, Henry VIII, and his second wife, Anne Boleyn. When Elizabeth was two years old, her mother was beheaded on the orders of her father. Elizabeth was sent away from court and brought up by tutors and governesses at Hatfield House in Hertfordshire.

In 1553, Mary I became queen. During the reign of Henry VIII, England had broken away from the Catholic Church. Mary, a devout Catholic, worked hard, and often ruthlessly, to make the country Catholic again. Protestants were often persecuted and killed. Elizabeth herself was imprisoned in the Tower of London on suspicion of leading a Protestant rebellion.

Learning to be queen

After two months in the Tower, Elizabeth was released. Mary sent her away from London to live in Woodstock, near Oxford, but kept her under guard. She was later allowed to move back to Hatfield House, where she had spent her childhood. It was here that Elizabeth heard of her sister's death on November 17, 1558. Elizabeth was now queen at only 25 years old. A week later, she returned to London to begin the task of ruling England.

Elizabeth's top priority was to make England a Protestant country again, while still allowing some of the old Catholic traditions to continue. She also appointed a group of trusted advisors to help her during her rule.

ELIZABETH'S ARMADA DIARY

January 15, 1559
Westminster Abbey, London
Today was the best day of my life — I was crowned Queen of England in Westminster Abbey. I had a fabulous new robe to wear and as the Bishop placed the crown on my head, trumpets sounded. I can't believe I'm Queen of England! What a day!

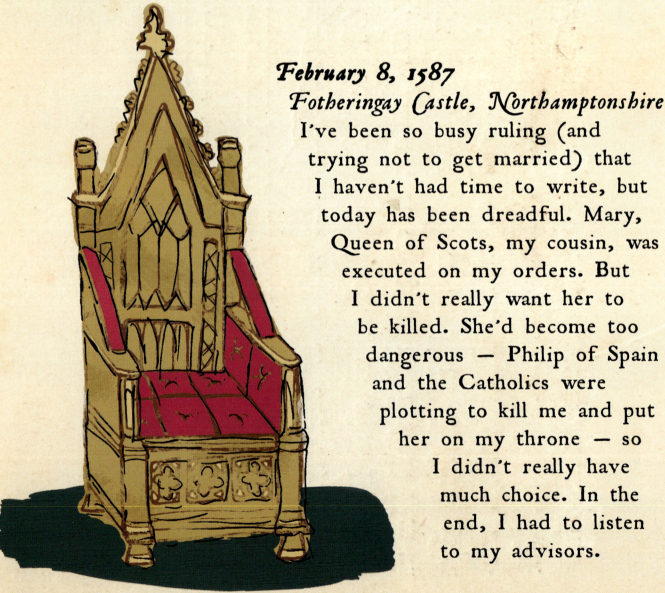

February 8, 1587
Fotheringay Castle, Northamptonshire
I've been so busy ruling (and trying not to get married) that I haven't had time to write, but today has been dreadful. Mary, Queen of Scots, my cousin, was executed on my orders. But I didn't really want her to be killed. She'd become too dangerous — Philip of Spain and the Catholics were plotting to kill me and put her on my throne — so I didn't really have much choice. In the end, I had to listen to my advisors.

July 19, 1588
Cornwall, southeast England
That fool Philip has sent an armada, a fleet of ships — 130 of them! — to attack England and pay me back for Mary's death. The ships were spotted off the coast, and beacons lit along the clifftops sent the news to London. He's not going to get away with this.

July 28, 1588
Calais, France
Brilliant news. The Spanish were anchored off Calais when Sir Francis Drake had an idea. He ordered eight old ships to be filled with wood, tar, and gunpowder. These were set on fire and sent off towards the Spanish ships. In a panic, the Spanish scattered and our warships were able to strike. That'll teach them.

August 9, 1588
Tilbury, London
I thought our forces needed a bit of encouragement so I went to Tilbury and gave a stirring speech. It was pretty good, though I say so myself. Even as I was speaking, the Spanish ships were battling their way through storms off Scotland. They won't be back in a hurry. We've won — hoorah!

COMMANDING QUEENS

Many powerful queens were loved by their subjects. During her reign, Elizabeth chose not to marry, saying that she was "married" to her country.

British and Armada ships

After the Armada

The failure of the Spanish Armada was a great victory for Elizabeth, but the following years saw economic problems for England. Elizabeth died in 1603 after a 45-year reign. She was the last of the Tudor monarchs.

Empress Wu Zetian

Wu Zetian married Emperor Gaozong and took control after his death in 683 CE. In 690, she became the first and only female Empress of China. During her peaceful and prosperous reign, she cut taxes and improved wages.

Empress Wu Zetian

Hermitage Museum, Russia, founded by Catherine the Great

Catherine the Great

Catherine became Empress of Russia when her husband, Grand Duke Peter, was overthrown in 1762. Under her rule, she expanded Russia's empire, and continued the process of modernization that was started by Peter the Great. She loved literature and education.

Timeline of female rulers

1478 BCE
Hatshepsut
Crowned Queen of Egypt and reigns for more than 20 years.

690 CE
Empress Wu Zetian
Becomes the first female Empress of China.

1588
Elizabeth I
Celebrates victory over the Spanish Armada.

1762
Catherine the Great
Becomes Empress of Russia and expands the country's empire.

1837
Queen Victoria
Crowned Queen of Britain and goes on to have the longest reign of any female monarch in history.

George Washington

Mr. President

Leader of the Continental Army in the American Revolution, George Washington was a brilliant soldier. After a stunning victory, he turned his attention to politics, becoming the first ever president of the United States and returning to serve for a second term.

Early life

Born on February 22, 1732, in Virginia, George was the eldest of six children. His well-to-do family owned tobacco plantations and hundreds of enslaved people. As a boy, George was taught at home by tutors, but he also learned how to grow crops, raise livestock, and look after the land.

When George was 11 years old, his father died and he was brought up by his half-brother, Lawrence. When Lawrence died in 1752, George inherited Mount Vernon, the large family estate on the banks of the Potomac River. It was to be his home for the rest of his life.

Going to war

At that time, parts of America called the colonies were ruled by the British and French. In 1754, war broke out between them for control of the borders between their lands. George was now a major in the Virginia militia (small army) and over the next few years, he fought bravely many times and was praised for his leadership and courage. In August 1755, he was made commander of the Virginia army. He was just 23 years old.

George left the army in 1758 and returned to Mount Vernon. He got married and devoted himself to family life and the estate. But he also began to get involved with the 13 British colonies, including Virginia, that wanted to be free from British rule. In April 1775, fighting broke out near Boston — the colonies were at war. The American Revolution had begun and George was to play a leading role.

WASHINGTON'S WARTIME DIARY

July 1775
Cambridge, Massachusetts
Exciting times! I've been made Commander-in-chief of the Continental Army to lead the revolt against the British. The army's made up of soldiers from all 13 colonies, and they're a bit of a ragtag bunch. It's my job to turn them into a top fighting force — wish me luck.

December 26, 1776
Delaware River
In August, we suffered a heavy defeat at the Battle of Long Island, and were forced to retreat. But things are looking up. Last night, we braved the ice and crossed the Delaware River into New Jersey to launch a surprise attack. The British never saw us coming and we captured almost a whole garrison. Morale is high.

October 19, 1781
Yorktown, Virginia
We've done it! The war is over and we've won! With help from the French, we attacked the British forces. The British, led by

Lord Cornwallis, held out as long as they could, but this morning they waved the white flag. We've just had the ceremony of surrender. Cornwallis didn't come — he's ill, apparently. So, I asked my second-in-command to accept the sword of surrender instead of me. Two can play at that game.

April 30, 1789
New York City

The proudest day of my life! I was sworn in as the first president of the United States and took the oath of office on the balcony of Federal Hall. A huge crowd came to cheer and there was a 13-gun salute. Afterwards, I gave my first speech in the Senate chamber. Being called "Mr. President" is going to take some getting used to.

September 19, 1796
Philadelphia, Pennsylvania

Today, my farewell address is in the newspaper. After two terms as president, I'm retiring next year. But before I go, I wanted to write a letter to the American people, setting out my ideas for our country. I have written about how vital it is to have unity among our states, a strong government, and for people to stay true to their values and take pride in being American.

IMPORTANT PRESIDENTS

George Washington is remembered as a great soldier, a skilful politician, and a man with a deep sense of patriotism. You can find out about some other notable presidents on these pages.

George Washington, 1732-97

First president
Washington helped to draw up the U.S. Constitution and, as the first president of the United States, he established many traditions that still continue today. Two years after his 1797 retirement, he caught a chill while inspecting his farmland and died a few days later.

Thomas Jefferson
One of the U.S. Founding Fathers, Jefferson drafted the Declaration of Independence in 1776. Passionate about democracy, he was elected president in 1801. In 1803, he bought land from France, doubling the size of the country.

Thomas Jefferson, who died in 1826

Charles de Gaulle depicted on a stamp

Charles de Gaulle
After World War I, Charles de Gaulle was promoted to leader of the French army. During World War II, he organized the resistance against German control of France. After the war, de Gaulle led the French government until 1946, and was president from 1958 until 1968.

Timeline of presidents

1789
George Washington
Becomes the first president of the United States.

1819
Thomas Jefferson
Former U.S. president founds the University of Virginia.

1940
Charles de Gaulle
Leader of France begins organizing the Free French movement during World War II.

1963
Jomo Kenyatta
Founding father of the Kenyan nation leads his country to independence and remains its leader until his death in 1978.

1991
Boris Yeltsin
Becomes first president of the Russian Federation.

Napoleon Bonaparte
Empire Builder

One of the greatest military leaders in history, Napoleon Bonaparte made a name for himself during the French Revolution. He became the first emperor of France and conquered large parts of Europe before his final famous defeat at Waterloo in 1815.

Becoming a soldier

Napoleon was born on August 15, 1769, on the island of Corsica (part of France). His father, Carlo, was a lawyer at the court of King Louis XVI, and the family was reasonably wealthy with good connections.

In 1779, Napoleon was sent to mainland France and enrolled at a military academy at Brienne-le-Château. There, he excelled at math, but was teased because he spoke French with a Corsican accent. His studies completed, Napoleon won a place at the École Militaire, a top military academy in Paris where he trained to be an artillery officer. In 1785, he became the first Corsican to graduate from the academy.

Rise to power

After graduating, Napoleon was made a second lieutenant in the French army, and was later promoted to captain. This was a turbulent time in France's history. In 1792, three years after the French Revolution began, France became a republic and, a year later, King Louis XVI was executed. Napoleon seized his chance. In return for helping the new government, he was made Commander of the French army in Italy, where he forced Austria to make peace with France.

Napoleon's next campaign was not so successful. This time, he set out to conquer Egypt, but his forces were destroyed by Admiral Nelson at the Battle of the Nile in 1798. It was a blow to Napoleon's reputation, but he was not down and out for long. In 1799, he overthrew the government and became the most powerful man in France.

BONAPARTE'S EMPIRE-BUILDING DIARY

June 14, 1800
Marengo, Italy
I came back to Italy to deal with some unfinished business — those pesky Austrians had been attacking our troops again. Anyway, we showed them. They won't forget the Battle of Marengo in a hurry. True, it didn't start off well. By early afternoon, they'd got us on the run, but we managed to reform and launch a surprise attack of our own.

December 2, 1804
Paris, France
Just when I thought things couldn't get any better, they did! I was already First Consul of France, but today, I was crowned emperor by the Pope. Now, I'm Napoleon I. The ceremony took place in Notre Dame. I wore a splendid robe of red velvet and fur, which was so heavy it needed four men to hold it up. I also had a brand-new crown made (the old one was destroyed during the Revolution).

December 2, 1805
Austerlitz, Moravia

I needed to lure the Austrians and Russians into battle so I came up with a cunning plan. I pretended that the French Army was on its last legs, and they fell for it — hook, line, and sinker. Then our troops swept through their ranks, taking thousands of prisoners. It was my greatest victory yet. Soon, all of Europe will be mine — I mean, will belong to France.

Sometime in April 1814
On the way to Elba

A terrible day. After a few disastrous campaigns, I've been forced to abdicate. I'm being exiled to Elba, some titchy island off the coast of Italy. Apparently, I'll be in charge there and even allowed to be called Emperor. Pah! Oh well, better start planning my escape.

June 18, 1815
Waterloo, Belgium

I managed to escape from Elba in March and travelled to Paris. Wish I hadn't bothered. Today was the worst day yet. At Waterloo, we were well and truly beaten by the British, led by the Duke of Wellington and his Prussian pals. Reckon it'll be my last battle. Wonder which godforsaken island they'll banish me to this time?

IMPOSING EMPERORS

Napoleon was a military genius who introduced many important reforms in France. Throughout history, empire-builders have often been gifted administrators as well as powerful personalities.

Napoleon Bonaparte, 1769–1821

The reformer

After the defeat at Waterloo, Napoleon was captured by the British and exiled to the island of St. Helena in the Atlantic ocean. He died there in 1821. His legacy is the reorganization of tax and education systems and the Napoleonic Code, a set of rules that still influence modern legal systems.

Qin Shi Huangdi

The first emperor of the Qin Dynasty, Qin Shi Huangdi oversaw many reforms and built roads and canals. After his death in 201 BCE, he was buried in a gigantic tomb protected by a vast army of life-sized terracotta warriors.

The terracotta army

Charlemagne, who died in 814 CE

Charlemagne

Charlemagne became king of the Franks in 768 CE and campaigned to extend his kingdom and spread Christianity. By 800 CE, he ruled most of western Europe. The Pope crowned him as the first emperor of the Holy Roman Empire — although he did not use the title.

Timeline of emperors

221 BCE
Qin Shi Huangdi
Conquers the Warring States to become the first emperor of the Qin Dynasty in China.

800 CE
Charlemagne
Crowned the first emperor in western Europe following the end of the Roman Empire in 800.

1206
Genghis Khan
Founder of the Mongol Empire begins leading the Mongol invasions that conquer huge areas of Asia.

1556
Akbar
Becomes ruler of the Mughal Empire and begins expansion of the empire to cover most of the Indian subcontinent.

1815
Napoleon Bonaparte
Finally defeated at the Battle of Waterloo in Belgium.

GLOSSARY

abdicate To formally give up power, office, or responsibility.

artillery Large firearms, such as canons.

diplomat A person who is skilled at talks between people or nations.

exile A situation in which someone is forced to leave their home or country to live in another place.

garrison A military post, as well as the soldiers stationed there.

pharaoh A ruler of ancient Egypt.

plantation A large Southern farm that used slave labor.

turbulent Causing or being in a state of unrest, violence, or disturbance.

FOR MORE INFORMATION

DK Publishing. *George Washington and the American Revolution.* London, UK: DK Children, 2025.

Melmoth, Jonathan. *Elizabeth I: Queen of England 1558-1603.* London, UK: DK Children, 2024.

Ramses II aka Ramses the Great
www.ancient-egypt-online.com/ramses-II.html

INDEX

Adolphus, Gustavus, 13
Akbar, 31

Bonaparte, Napoleon, 7, 26, 27, 28, 29, 30, 31

Catherine the Great, 18, 19

Charlemagne, 30, 31

de Gaul, Charles, 24, 25

Elizabeth I, 6, 14, 15, 16, 17, 18, 19
Empress Wu Zetian, 18, 19

Frederick II, 13

Hatshepsut, 19

Jefferson, Thomas, 24, 25

Ramesses II, 6, 8, 9, 10, 11, 12, 13

Washington, George, 7, 20, 21, 22, 23, 24, 25

Zulu, Shaka, 12, 13